WHAT IS PHILOSOPHY?

What is Philosophy?

Michael Munro

dead letter office

BABEL Working Group

punctum books ✶ brooklyn, ny

WHAT IS PHILOSOPHY?
© Michael Munro, 2012.

This work is licensed under the Creative Commons Attribution-NonCommercial-NoDerivs 3.0 Unported License. To view a copy of this license, visit: http://creativecommons.org/licenses/by-nc-nd/3.0, or send a letter to Creative Commons, 444 Castro Street, Suite 900, Mountain View, California, 94041, USA.

This work is Open Access, which means that you are free to copy, distribute, display, and perform the work as long as you clearly attribute the work to the authors, that you do not use this work for commercial gain in any form whatsoever, and that you in no way alter, transform, or build upon the work outside of its normal use in academic scholarship without express permission of the author and the publisher of this volume. For any reuse or distribution, you must make clear to others the license terms of this work.

First published in 2012 by
Dead Letter Office, BABEL Working Group
an imprint of punctum books
Brooklyn, New York

The BABEL Working Group is a collective and desiring-assemblage of scholar-gypsies with no leaders or followers, no top and no bottom, and only a middle. BABEL roams and stalks the ruins of the post-historical university as a multiplicity, a pack, looking for other roaming packs and multiplicities with which to cohabit and build temporary shelters for intellectual vagabonds. We also take in strays.

ISBN-10: 0615685137
ISBN-13: 978-0615685137

Library of Congress Cataloging-in-Publication Data is available from the Library of Congress.

to s.o.

TABLE OF CONTENTS

What is Philosophy?	1
On Argument	7
On Not Knowing	22
Notes	33
References	55

What is Philosophy?

Michael Munro

 What is Philosophy?

§ The Place of the Question: Note on the Definition of Philosophy

What is philosophy? That's a good question—not because there's no answer, but because what's involved in posing it points up something essential to philosophy.

In the *Treatise on the Emendation of the Intellect*, Spinoza sets out what's required by a definition. A circle, a typical definition might run, is a figure in which all lines drawn from the center to the circumference are equal. The problem with this definition, what makes it merely verbal, is that it defines a circle by way of one of its properties, not by way of its essence. Definition, for Spinoza, gets at the essence (from which all properties follow): A complete definition demonstrates how what it defines comes about. The definition of a circle as a figure that is described by any line of which one end is fixed and the other movable, as one commentator has pointed out, "literally generates the circle by providing a procedure whereby we 'make' the thing to be defined."[1]

Philosophy is defined by what takes place in the question of philosophy itself. What Auden said of poetry could also be said of philosophy: it makes nothing happen. *Nothing* happens, or nothing *happens*—and in the space of the same few words both *can*. Philosophy operates that displacement and is defined by it: "what is *philosophy?*" become "*what is* philosophy?"—the question persists, but everything has changed.

§ What is Philosophy? Gloss of a Sentence of Giorgio Agamben's

"In its deepest intention, philosophy is a firm assertion of potentiality, the construction of an experience of the possible as such."

in its deepest intention

Philosophy, it is said, begins in wonder. *Wonder,*

---

[1] Bibliographic references for all citations can be found under "Notes" at the back of the book, keyed to page numbers in the main body of this essay.

however, is both a noun and a verb. Noun: "A feeling of surprise mingled with admiration, caused by something beautiful, unexpected, unfamiliar, or inexplicable." Verb: "The desire, or curiosity, to know something."

philosophy is

In that light, philosophy is not so much—or not simply—'the love of wisdom,' but instead marks the passage from wonder as a noun to wonder as a verb. Philosophy is the love of wisdom to the extent that it remains an incitement to it.

a firm assertion

To philosophize has often been to argue. 'Argument' comes from the Latin *arguere*, to make clear. To argue might then be said to mean *to give an idea of, to clarify*. In the very divergence of the arguments used and the positions held, what argument and the recourse to it in philosophy testify to before all else—what they clarify—is, precisely, the nature of the possible.

of potentiality

Potentiality and possibility alike concern ability or capacity: *what may be*. 'A firm assertion of potentiality,' is, in the first place, an affirmation of the importance of *what may be* to *what is*. *What is* is not what it is without what it may be, or may have been. Likewise, and after its own fashion, what may be *is*. Wonder enters the picture between potentiality and actuality, and philosophy affirms their articulation: Surprised admiration at what is gives place to what had not yet existed, the desire to know it.

the construction of

To construct is a transitive verb, which means that *to construct* is always to construct *something*. It is to take something that is given and to make of it something that was not, something it was not, something else. It is to take something as it is for something it may be.

an experience

Experience shares the same root as *experiment*.

of the possible as such

Neither this nor that possibility, but possibility in general, what makes the possible what it is: What there is not, yet, beyond the desire, its experience: what it might be *to know*.

§ PHILOSOPHY: A LIFE...

There is a tradition according to which philosophy is known as 'the art of living.' That definition of philosophy only finds its true sense, however, and not coincidentally, in light of a definition of potentiality first elaborated at philosophy's outset.

As Giorgio Agamben recounts, Aristotle opposes his definition of potentiality to that of the Megarians. Whereas the Megarians hold that in a given act all potentiality passes into actuality, so that nothing is left over in this passage and potentiality has no independent existence as such, Aristotle holds that potentiality is distinct from actuality and exists on a par with it. At issue between Aristotle and the Megarians is the example of the kithara player. The problem with the Megarians' position, for Aristotle, is that it fails to distinguish someone who can play the kithara from someone who cannot: on their account it is impossible to say why when one person picks up a kithara she can make music with it while another person cannot. If all potentiality passes immediately and without remainder into actuality, there's simply music or there's not.

That consideration leads Aristotle to make what at first glance appears to be a counterintuitive observation: The difference between someone who can play the kithara and someone who cannot is that the kithara player is *capable* of *not playing* the kithara. The real difference between the two takes place, paradoxically, away from the instrument. The kithara player can be said to be capable of not playing the kithara in a way that it would not make sense to say of someone who is simply incapable of playing it: for the latter, away from the kithara, entertains no relation to it and, to him or her, that absence is a matter of indifference. What is essential to the kithara player's potential to play the kithara, and what for Aristotle is essential to potentiality more generally, is that what he calls *the impotential* to do, or be, something is what remains of potentiality that never passes into actuality and serves to distinguish the former from the latter.

In any given instance to be capable of an impotentiality is therefore to be able to be affected by the absence, following cessation, of the activity in question. It is to be one to whom that absence makes a difference.

Philosophy is the art of living in that to be a philosopher is to first be capable of the non-philosophical life. To be a philosopher is to feel the absence of the philosophical life bear on one's own.

 ON ARGUMENT

§ Preface: Note Toward an Art of Ignorance

It is very difficult to say why one becomes attached to a particular problem.
~Gilles Deleuze

Samuel Taylor Coleridge opens Chapter 12 of the *Biographia Literaria* with curious resolve. "In the perusal of philosophical works I have been greatly benefited by a resolve, which, in the antithetic form and with the allowed quaintness of an adage or maxim, I have been accustomed to word thus: '*until you understand a writer's ignorance, presume yourself ignorant of his understanding.*'" What is the relationship posed here between ignorance and understanding?

In *Memoirs of the Blind*, Jacques Derrida discusses the conditions and status of self-portraiture. According to Derrida, "the status of the self-portrait of the self-portraitist will always retain a hypothetical character." "Even if one were sure," for example, "that Fantin-Latour were drawing himself drawing, one would never know, *observing the work alone*, whether he were showing himself drawing *himself* or *something else*—or even himself *as something else, as other*. And he can always, in addition, draw this situation: the stealing away of what regards you, of what looks at you, of what fixedly observes you not seeing that with which or with whom you are dealing." None of that can be known for a very general reason: In the instant pen or pencil makes contact with paper, "the inscription of the inscribable is not seen." Further,

> Whether it be improvised or not, the invention of the *trait* [trait, feature, line, stroke, mark] does not follow, it does not conform to what is presently visible [...] Even if drawing is, as they say, mimetic, that is, reproductive, figurative, representative, even if the model is presently facing the artist, the *trait* must proceed in the night. It escapes the field of vision. Not only because it *is not yet* visible, but because it does not belong to the realm of the spectacle, of spectacular objectivity—and so that which it makes happen or come [*advenir*] cannot in itself be mimetic. [...] Whether one underscores this with the words of Plato or Merleau-Ponty, the visibility of the visible cannot, by definition, be seen, no more than what Aristotle speaks of as the diaphanousness of light can be. My hypothesis—remember that we are still within the logic of the hypothesis—is that the draftsman always sees himself to be prey

to that which is each time universal and singular and would have to be called the *unbeseen*, as one speaks of the unbeknownst.

In order to be read—in order to be worth having read—above all one must unknowingly have preserved for another an ignorance to be understood. One can perhaps paraphrase Benjamin here and speak of an historical index proper to ignorance, that it only attains to legibility as such at a particular time, that of its recognizability.

A situation, indeed. To be made to glimpse "what fixedly observes you not seeing that with which or with whom you are dealing": I draw on the ignorance of others in order to have drawn, with my own ignorance, my own self-portrait.

§ ON ARGUMENT: FRAGMENTS

Alfred North Whitehead: "It is more important that a proposition be interesting than that it be true. The importance of truth," he goes on to say, "is that it adds to interest."

In 1735, with the first appearance of the *Systema naturae*, Linnaeus assigns *Homo* to the order of the *Anthropomorpha*. From the tenth edition of 1758 on, that order will be called *Primates*. "In truth, Linnaeus' genius consists not so much in the resoluteness with which he places man among the primates," Giorgio Agamben has commented,

> as in the irony with which he does not record—as he does with the other species—any specific identifying characteristic next to the generic name *Homo*, only the old philosophical adage: *nosce te ipsum* [know yourself]. Even in the tenth edition, when the complete denomination becomes *Homo sapiens*, all evidence suggests that the new epithet does not represent a description, but that it is only a simplification of the adage, which, moreover, maintains its position next to the term *Homo*. It is worth reflecting on this taxonomic anomaly, which assigns not a given, but rather an imperative as a specific difference.
>
> An analysis of the *Introitus* that opens the *Systema* leaves no doubts about the sense Linnaeus attributed to his maxim: man has no specific identity other than the *ability* to recognize himself. Yet to define the human not through any *nota characteristica*, but rather through his self-knowledge, means that man is the being which recognizes itself as such, that *man is the animal that must recognize itself as human to be human.*

Amid the backlash, Agamben continues, "the notes for a reply to another critic, Theodor Klein, show how far Linnaeus was willing to push the irony implicit in the formula *Homo sapiens*. Those who, like Klein, do not recognize themselves in the position that the *Systema* has assigned to man should apply the *nosce te ipsum* to themselves; in not knowing how to recognize themselves as man, they have placed themselves among the apes."

And yet it is significant that this reply is elaborated only in notes. On his own terms, and in principle, Linnaeus could not make that response. *Homo* is, again in Agamben's words, "a constitutively 'anthropomorphous' animal": Man only *resembles* man, and in order to recognize himself for what he is, he must recognize himself as merely one among the *Anthropomorpha*. Linnaeus could not make that response to his critics, in other words, because he had staked his humanity on recognizing himself in them—in those, precisely, who are unable to.

Hume only became who he is because he managed to wake one philosopher from his dogmatic slumber. It's entirely possible he may yet wake more. Should he do so it will be in no small part thanks to the work of Quentin Meillassoux: he has added his voice to Hume's and revived the latter's problem in all its radicality. Hume asks how we know the future will resemble the past, that is, that the usual connections observed between successive events are necessary and, in fact, universal. The short answer? We can't. Hume's treatment of the problem presaged its subsequent treatment from his time until today: because we believe in causal necessity on the basis of habit, induction has largely been treated as a practical problem, in other words, and for example, under what conditions and by what means are inductive inferences generally made? In its ontological dimension the problem is taken to be insoluble because where it leads is taken to be absurd. Not so, Meillassoux:

> On the contrary, the ontological approach I speak of would consist in affirming that it is possible rationally to envisage that the constants could effectively change *for no reason whatsoever*, and thus with no necessity whatsoever; which, as I will insist, leads us to envisage a contingency so radical that it would incorporate all conceivable futures of the present laws, *including that consisting in the absence of their modification*.

Meillassoux continues, "I would affirm that, indeed, there is no reason for phenomenal constants to be constant. I maintain, then, that

> these laws could change. One thereby circumvents what, in induction, usually gives rise to the problem: the proof, on

the basis of past experience, of the future constancy of laws. But one encounters another difficulty, which appears at least as redoubtable: if laws have no reason to be constant, *why do they not change at each and every instant*? If a law is what it is purely contingently, it could change at any moment. The persistence of the laws of the universe seems consequently to break all laws of probability: for if the laws are effectively contingent, it seems that they must frequently manifest such contingency. If the duration of laws does not rest upon any necessity, it must be a function of successive 'dice rolls', falling each time in favour of their continuation [...]. From this point of view, their manifest perenniality becomes a probabilistic aberration—and it is precisely because we never observe such modifications that such a hypothesis has seemed, to those who tackled the problem of induction, too absurd to be seriously envisaged.

If "the persistence of the laws of the universe seems consequently to break all laws of probability," Meillassoux goes on to argue, that's because probability doesn't apply here. To the objection that the uniformity of nature would be tantamount to untold dice throws with the same result, Žižek has pointed out that

that argument "relies on a possible totalization of possibilities/probabilities, *with regard to which* the uniformity is improbable: if there is no standard, nothing is more improbable than anything else." And that is very precisely the case here: there can be no standard in principle because the universe, unlike a die or a coin, possesses no denumerable set of possible states, no delimitable set of inherent possibilities. That is to say, the universe is nontotalizable. And it may even be illegitimate for that reason to speak of '*the* universe.' Umberto Eco has discussed this point near the end of "The Power of Falsehood." "Does the universe exist? Good question." If the universe does not exist that's because the future does.

Argument is by nature a rearguard action. (Nietzsche: "—what have I to do with refutations!—"; "I refute it *thus*": and thus Dr. Johnson kicks the stone but misses Berkeley.) The emphasis—the interest—is elsewhere: as Deleuze and Guattari put it, lines of flight are primary. First you flee, and only in flight do you fashion a weapon.

§ Addendum: On Argument

"Philosophy," Quentin Meillassoux has stated, "is the invention of strange forms of argumentation." A curious claim, it is at the same time a profound intuition. What's at stake for philosophy in the changing forms of argumentation employed in it, and according to what necessity does the recourse to invention impose itself there?

Alexander Nehamas has staged the divided desire that organizes Nietzsche's work. Nietzsche "wants, on the one hand, to distinguish himself from Socrates and from the philosophical tradition. One way in which he might have achieved this goal would have been

> to refrain from writing anything that might in any conceivable manner be construed as philosophical—the only certain method of accomplishing this purpose being to refrain from writing altogether. But this is not, and cannot be, Nietzsche's way. Refraining from writing, assuming that this was something he had any choice about, would not simply have distinguished him from the tradition; it would have prevented him from being related to it in any way. But Nietzsche also wants, on the other hand, to criticize that tradition and to offer views of his own which, in their undogmatic manner, will compete with other views. Yet this procedure always involves the risk of falling back into the philosophical tradition after all. We can think of philosophy as a mirror in which those who belong to it are reflected, while those

who are not reflected are totally irrelevant to it.

Argument, above all, and before any explicit contention, registers the effects of a departure—and that nowhere more so than in its form. Formal invention in argumentation obliquely describes, in philosophy, the limit that joins what is relevant to what is irrelevant to philosophy. Wanting, strangely, it will have broached it in reflection.

§ Untimely Meditations

Without question, philosophy is an activity. One "does" philosophy; one philosophizes. What remains an open question, however, is the character and status of that activity: What is it to philosophize? In other words, what does one do when one does philosophy?

1.

In Chapter XV, "The Value of Philosophy," the concluding chapter of *The Problems of Philosophy*, Bertrand Russell observes that, "Philosophy, like all other studies, aims primarily at knowledge." "But," he immediately concedes, "it cannot be maintained that philosophy has had any great measure of success in its attempts to provide definite answers to its questions. If you ask a mathematician, a mineralogist, a historian, or any other man [*sic* throughout] of learning, what definite body of truths has been ascertained by his science, his answer will last

> as long as you are willing to listen. But if you put the same question to a philosopher, he will, if he is candid, have to confess that his study has not achieved positive results such as have been achieved by other sciences. It is true that this is partly accounted for by the fact that, as soon as definite knowledge concerning any subject becomes possible, this subject ceases to be called philosophy, and becomes a separate science. The whole study of the heavens, which now belongs to astronomy, was once included in philosophy; Newton's great work was called 'the mathematical principles of natural philosophy.' Similarly, the study of the human mind, which was a part of philosophy, has now been separated from philosophy and has become the science of psychology. Thus, to a great extent, the uncertainty of philosophy is more apparent than real: those questions which are already capable of definite answers are placed in the sciences, while those only to which, at present, no definite answer can be given, remain to form the residue which is called philosophy.

2.

What remains, at present, to form that "residue which is called philosophy"? Perhaps nothing more, nor less, finally, than what philosophy ever had.

Eric Dietrich has claimed that philosophy does not progress, that it "is exactly the same today as it was 3000 years ago; indeed, as it was from the beginning. What it does do," however, he goes on to contend, "is stay current":

> Imagine that Aristotle, as he's walking around the Lyceum, encounters a time-warp and pops forward to today, on a well-known campus somewhere in some English-speaking country, with the ability to speak English, dressed in modern garb, and that he doesn't become deranged as a result of all this. Curious about the state of knowledge, he finds a physics lecture and sits in. What he hears shocks him. A feather and an iron ball fall at the same rate in a vacuum; being heavier doesn't mean falling faster, something he doesn't understand. Aristotle along with the rest of the class is shown the experimental verification of this from the moon (*from the moon*?!?!?) performed by Commander David Scott of Apollo 15. The very same equations (*equations*?!?!?) that explain why an apple falls to the

ground explain how the moon stays in orbit around Earth and how Earth stays in orbit around the sun (*orbits*?!?!?). He learns of quantum mechanics' strangenesses. The more he hears, the more shocked he gets. Finally, he just faints away. He faints away again in cosmology class where he learns, for starters, that comets and meteors, and the Milky Way are not atmospheric phenomena, as he concluded. The Big Bang, relativity, the size of the universe, the number of galaxies, dark matter, and dark energy . . . are all too much for him. In biology class, he learns that a living thing's *potential*, its matter, is not at all explanatory, as he thought, but instead learns of genetics and developmental biology. He also learns that his idea of spontaneous generation is just plain wrong—not even close to being correct. He learns of evolution and the discovery that all of life on Earth is related. As the class continues, he again faints dead away.

After he comes to, he soberly concludes that this modern world, this advanced time, has utterly surpassed his knowledge and the knowledge of his time. He feels dwarfed by our epistemic sophistication. Sadly, he trundles off to a philosophy class—a metaphysics class, as it turns out. Here he hears the professor lecturing about essences, about being qua being, about the most general structures of our thinking about the world. He knows exactly what the professor is talking about. Aristotle raises his hand to discuss some errors the professor seems to have made, and some important distinctions that he has not drawn. As the discussion proceeds, the metaphysics professor is a bit taken aback but also delighted at this (older) student's acumen and insight. Then Aristotle goes to an ethics class, where he learns of the current importance of what is apparently called "virtue ethics." He recognizes it immediately, but again, the professor seems to have left out some crucial details and failed to see some deeper aspects of the view. Aristotle raises his hand. . .

This story of Aristotle's return to philosophy no doubt is somewhat plausible to the reader (excluding, probably, the time-travel part). Perhaps it is no more than that or just barely that. But this is all I need.

3.

Gilles Deleuze has developed a theory of the event, of what constitutes an event. In contrast to the classical conception according to which being is opposed to becoming as eternity is to time, Deleuze opposes becoming to history: whereas becoming is classically identified with history, it is their difference, their noncoincidence, that pertains to events. As Deleuze has it, "not exactly something that occurs, but something *in* that which occurs," "the part that eludes its own actualization in everything that happens."

An activity that approximates inactivity, an event that to all appearances approaches a nonoccurrence, what one does when one does philosophy is, against history, *to become*—"that is to say, acting counter to our time and thereby acting on our time and, let us hope, for a time to come."

ON NOT KNOWING

§ A Defense of the Unknowable

1.

From a commentary generalizing an argument against Kant's thing-in-itself to include "any theory of an unknowable":

> What is meant in philosophy by the unknowable is something which, apart from all accidental circumstances, is such that the constitution of our minds is radically incapable of knowing it, something which is totally outside any conceivable human knowledge, some-thing from which we are completely cut off, not by distance or lack of instruments and the like, but by the nature of our mental processes.
>
> If anything is unknowable, this means that it is absolutely unknowable. And if we have any knowledge of it, however slight, it is not unknowable.
>
> Total ignorance of a thing involves total unawareness of it, and therefore it involves unawareness of our ignorance.

Let us straightaway concede it all. But in what then does this defense consist? What is there left to save?

2.

A first approach to the unknowable may be to take note of the suffix, *-able*: in English it denotes a capacity, an ability or capability—a potentiality. But what is a capacity? How is one to conceive of its existence? And how does it subsist in its exercise, its realization?

A clue can be found in an obscure passage of the *De Anima*: "To suffer is not a simple term," Aristotle writes. Further,

> In one sense it is a certain destruction through the opposite principle, and in another sense it is the preservation [*sōtēria*, salvation] of what is in potentiality by what is in actuality and what is similar to it. . . . For he who possesses science [in potentiality] becomes someone who contemplates in actuality, and either this is not an alteration—since here there is the gift of the self to itself and to actuality [*epidosiseis auto*]—or this is an alteration of a different kind.

"Contrary to the traditional idea of potentiality that is annulled in actuality," Giorgio Agamben has commented, "here we are confronted with a potentiality that conserves itself and saves itself in actuality. Here potentiality, so to speak, survives actuality"—and that by way of a "gift," "the gift of the self to itself *and* to actuality": At the limit, in the instant of passage, that gift is one and the same and potentiality is realized for what it *is*.

Despite tradition, Aristotle is in agreement with Spinoza when the latter maintains that there is no potentiality separate from actuality (as Aristotle had it, between them, either there is not an alteration, or it is an alteration of a different kind). Gilles Deleuze has provided the decisive clarification. "All *potentia*," for Spinoza, "is act, active and actual. The identity of power and action is explained by the following: all power is inseparable from a capacity for being affected, and this capacity for being affected is constantly and necessarily filled by affections that realize it." Potentiality adheres in actuality, capacity in its exercise, because it is as such ceaselessly active in it, affected by it without reprieve: Potentiality is actual in perpetually separating from itself the passage to actuality in order to preserve, with each instant, the jointure between them.

3.

But what of the prefix, *un*-? How might negation qualify a capacity?

Maurice Merleau-Ponty speculates on this

point in his notes:

> To touch and to touch oneself (to touch oneself = touching-touched [*touchant-touché*]). They do not coincide in the body: the touching is never exactly the touched. This does not mean that they coincide 'in the mind' or at the level of 'consciousness.' There must be something other than the body for the junction to be made. It is made in the *untouchable*. That which belongs to the Other which I will never touch. But that which I will never touch, he too does not touch; no privilege of the self over the other here. It is therefore not *consciousness* that is untouchable—'consciousness' would be something positive, and then there would be another beginning, there is another beginning, of the duality of the reflecting and the reflected, like that of the touching and the touched. The untouchable is not a touchable that happens to be inaccessible; the unconscious is not a representation that happens to be inaccessible. The negative here is not a *positive that is elsewhere* (something transcendent). It is a true negative.

Daniel Heller-Roazen has provided a beautiful commentary on this passage. It's worth quoting at length:

This note can be read as a compressed effort to explain a single fact: that however intimately they may be joined in a tactile act committed by one body on itself, the touching and the touched 'do not coincide.' Even when I lay one hand upon the other, the touching member, in other words, 'is never exactly the touched.' A medium, no matter how subtle it may seem, must separate the two tactile terms, even as it grants them the element in which they may meet.

Merleau-Ponty names this medium 'the untouchable.' Irreducible both to the felt body and to the mind, conscious or unconscious, it constitutes the indistinct terrain in which the junction between the touching and the touched comes to pass. As Merleau-Ponty defines it in his note, such an 'untouchable' is, quite clearly, withdrawn from tactility not accidentally but essentially. 'It is not a touchable that happens to be inaccessible,' the philosopher therefore specifies with pedagogical precision. It is 'not a positive that is elsewhere (something transcendent)' but 'a true negative.' There can be no doubt: the untouchable, for this reason, retreats from the field of touch in allowing it. But such a summary nevertheless runs the risk of philosophical inadequacy, for the nature of the untouchable medium of touch is in fact still more complex. The truth of the matter is that every touching and touched term solicits and encounters this element, precisely as that 'in which' all contact comes to pass; every grasp, be it forceful or gentle, exerts itself upon it and within it. Despite its structural inaccessibility, the medium of touch is therefore not impassive; in Merleau-Ponty's words, it is not 'something transcendent.' One might even maintain that, since no contact is immediate and 'the touching is never exactly the touched,' one never truly encounters anything but it. The ultimate element of all touch, it remains no less untouchable for being incessantly, always, and already touched.

A true negative, the capacity at issue in the untouchable and the unknowable alike finds its exercise in the non-coincidence between touching and touched, knowing and known: The excess of capacity in act, a solicitation and an encounter, it is the contact of the two terms *at* a remove.

4.

As to the root word *to know*, the unknowable is preserved in it to the extent that it is not known—it remains unclear whether it can be known—what it is, in principle, to know.

The unknowable is the gift of knowability. In that gift it is saved.

§ On Not Knowing

What moves me to write this is a perplexity. In order to effectively communicate that perplexity, free of confusion, let me attempt to delineate it by way of an example.

Two ways of not knowing?

Perhaps not any example, its classic formulation is to be found in Plato's *Meno* (80d-e):

> *Socrates*: [...] So now I do not know what virtue is; perhaps you knew before you contacted me, but now you are certainly like one who does not know. Nevertheless, I want to examine and seek together with you what it may be.
>
> *Meno*: How will you look for it, Socrates, when you do not know at all what it is? How will you aim to search for something you do not know at all? If you should meet with it, how will you know that this is the thing that you did not know?
>
> *Socrates*: I know what you want to say, Meno. Do you realize what a debater's argument you are bringing up, that a

man cannot search either for what he knows or for what he does not know? He cannot search for what he knows—since he knows it, there is no need to search—nor for what he does not know, for he does not know what to search for.

Is there a way for one not to know that is not simply not knowing? What would it be to become capable of it?

Taken to its extreme, what is at issue here is nothing less than the Socratic enterprise: How could Socrates know, as he puts it, that he knows nothing? What is that knowledge such that, for him, it instigates a "search" that is in every respect unprecedented? What, in light of that search, is the "nothing" that he knows?

In Place of Conclusion

What is an absence? If a given absence can be determined to be relevant to that to which it is nonetheless said to be absent, is it fair to maintain that it is in fact absent to it? And conversely, if an absence does not bear on anything, how can it be an absence?

Kant distinguishes between threshold (*Grenze*) and limit (*Schranke*). A threshold marks a passage, a delimitation that serves to join to something an outside that alters it, while a limit operates on that which it bounds by remaining, with respect to it, invisible. A limit never appears as such.

Of what relevance is perplexity? It is perhaps in this instance the sounding of a limit.

§ For the Love of Wisdom: Note

It's clear that "philosophy" comes from the Greek *philosophia*, love of wisdom. What's not at all clear is what that phrase means. In the connection it articulates between love and wisdom, what, precisely, does philosophy name?

In Chapter 4 of *The Open*, "*Mysterium disiunctionis*," Giorgio Agamben has discussed the manner in which, in the *De anima*, Aristotle defines "life":

> It is through life [Aristotle writes] that what has soul in it differs from what has not. Now this term 'to live' has more than one sense, and provided any one of these is found in a thing we say that the thing is living—viz. thinking, sensation, local movement and rest, or movement in the sense of nutrition, decay and growth. Hence we think of all species of plants also as living, for they are observed to possess in themselves a principle and potentiality through which they grow and decay in opposite directions. . . . This principle can be separated from the others, but not they from it—in mortal beings at least.

The fact is obvious in plants; for it is the only psychic potentiality they possess. Thus, it is through this principle that life belongs to living things. . . . By nutritive power we mean that part of the soul which is common also to plants.

It is important to observe that Aristotle in no way defines what life is: he limits himself to breaking it down, by isolating the nutritive function, in order then to rearticulate it in a series of distinct and correlated faculties or potentialities (nutrition, sensation, thought). Here we see at work the principle of foundation which constitutes the strategic device par excellence of Aristotle's thought. It consists in reformulating every question concerning 'what something is' as a question concerning 'through what something belongs to another thing.' To ask why a certain being is called living means to seek out the foundation by which living belongs to this being. That is to say, among the various senses of the term 'to live,' one must be separated from the others and settle to the bottom, becoming the principle by which life can be attributed to a certain being. In other words, what has been separated and divided (in this case nutritive life) is precisely what—in a sort of *divide et imperia*—allows the unity of life as the

> hierarchical articulation of a series of functional faculties and oppositions.

To paraphrase part of the analysis with which Agamben closes the chapter: What would it be to think philosophy not as the conjunction of love with wisdom but rather, following Aristotle's procedure, "as what results from the incongruity of these two elements"?

Is it permissible to speculate that philosophy may name a like disjunction, similarly mysterious?

What wisdom would there be in that? What love would it betray?

Notes

What Is Philosophy?

Pg. 1: What is philosophy? Gilles Deleuze and Felix Guattari, *What is Philosophy?* trans. Hugh Tomlinson and Graham Burchell (New York: Columbia University Press, 1994), 41: "The nonphilosophical is perhaps closer to the heart of philosophy than philosophy itself, and this means that philosophy cannot be content to be understood only philosophically or conceptually, but is addressed essentially to nonphilosophers as well."

Pg. 2: Definition, for Spinoza, gets at the essence Baruch Spinoza, *Ethics, Treatise on the Emendation of the Intellect, and Selected Letters*, ed. Seymour Feldman, trans. Samuel Shirley (Indianapolis: Hackett Publishing Company, Inc., 1992), 257–59, pars. 95–97.

Pg. 2: as one commentator has pointed out Seymour Feldman, Introduction to Baruch Spinoza,

Treatise on the Emendation of the Intellect, in *Ethics, Treatise on the Emendation of the Intellect, and Selected Letters*, ed. Feldman, 229.

Pg. 2: What Auden said of poetry W.H. Auden, *Collected Poems: Auden*, ed. Edward Mendelson (New York: Vintage, 1991), 246: "For poetry makes nothing happen: it survives / In the valley of its making […] it survives, / A way of happening, a mouth."

Pg. 2: it makes nothing happen

SUSPENSE: NOTE ON TOPOGRAPHY

The refutation of utopia, in politics as in philosophy, has proven no more definitive than has its invocation. That it remains an issue, however, affords a better understanding of it: its mode of persistence gives insight into its nature.

As Giorgio Agamben has recounted, a technical term of the Skeptics' stakes out a no man's land between affirmation and negation, acceptance and rejection: *ou mallon*, no more than. It is by way of this phrase that the Skeptics denote—and enact—what Agamben calls "their most characteristic experience," that of *epochē*, suspension: It is used by them to refute an argument at the same time as the counterargument on offer. "'No more than,'" records Diogenes Laertius, "is no more than it is not." Sextus Empiricus concurs. "Even as the proposition 'every discourse is false' says that it too, like all propositions, is false, so the formula 'no more than' says that it itself is no more than it is not."

Utopia exists no more than it does not exist. It has become a commonplace to point out that the word "utopia" originally designated "nowhere." But it is necessary to add what Gilles Deleuze observes of the title of Samuel Butler's utopian novel *Erewhon*: It is "not only a disguised *no-where* but a rearranged *now-here*." The reversibility of *no-where* and *now-here*—by way of a single, finally unlocatable space—makes of utopia the most common place. Giorgio Agamben, *Potentialities: Collected Essays in Philosophy*, ed. and trans. Daniel Heller-Roazen (Stanford: Stanford University Press, 1999), 256; Gilles Deleuze, *Difference and Repetition*, trans. Paul Patton (New York: Columbia University Press, 1994), 333n7.

Pg. 2: In its deepest intention, philosophy is Agamben, *Potentialities*, 249.

Pg. 4: the construction of In a recent interview Quentin Meillassoux has differentiated two senses of the word 'construction': "If I employ this word in connection with the work of an architect,

> what I mean is that the building thereby

constructed would not have existed without the architect's plan or the labour of the workers. But let's suppose that by 'construction' I refer instead to the mechanisms by which an archeologist has set up a dig site in order to excavate some ruins without damaging them. In this case the 'constructions' (a complex of winches, sounding lines, scaffolding, spades, brushes, etc.) are not destined to *produce* an object, as in the case of architecture. On the contrary, they are made with a view to *not* interfering with the object at which they aim: that is to say, excavating the ruins without damaging them.

Included in Graham Harman, *Quentin Meillassoux: Philosophy in the Making* (Edinburgh: Edinburgh University Press, 2011), 167.

Pg. 5: As Giorgio Agamben recounts Agamben has recounted Aristotle's definition of potentiality many times, prominent among them in "On Potentiality," in *Potentialities*, 177–84, and in *Homo Sacer: Sovereign Power and Bare Life*, trans. Daniel Heller-Roazen (Stanford: Stanford University Press, 1998), 44–47. "I could state the subject of my work," Agamben writes near the beginning of the former, "as an attempt to understand the meaning of the verb 'can' [*potere*]. What do I mean when I say: 'I can, I cannot?'" ("On Potentiality," 177). In a parenthetical interjection among his opening remarks in *The Neutral*, Roland Barthes proposes an interesting complication of that question when he writes, "(Who can distinguish between inability and the lack of taste?)" Roland Barthes, *The Neutral*, trans. Rosalind E. Krauss and Denis Hollier (New York: Columbia University Press, 2005), 10. Stated positively, how is taste implicated in ability? And what would it say of one's own ability, not to mention taste, going forward, to attempt to tease them apart?

On Argument

Pg. 7 On Argument

Apologia pro Vita Philosophicus, Apologia pro Vita Sua

In "Philosophy and Disagreement," Brian Ribeiro takes as his point of departure the question, "*Why*," in philosophy, "is there all this disagreement?":

> Philosophy is not only rife with disagreement; one might even say that philosophy is in the *business* of disagreement. That's who we are, or what we do, *qua* philosophers: we question, dispute, object, oppose, beg to differ, quibble, and sometimes even cavil. Since this is so, one might expect philosophy would, long ago, have

worked out a fairly sophisticated account of disagreement—of its nature, origin(s), and its implications for the practice of philosophy—but it seems fairly clear to me that this is not so.

I find that very surprising. After all, one of the other things philosophy is in the business of is being a thoroughly and uncompromisingly *self-critical* enterprise, i.e. being an enterprise that not only thinks about its paradigmatic objects of inquiry but also thinks about *itself* and *its relation* to its own inquiries. Thus, one might be surprised to find that philosophy is in the business of doing (at least) two things (viz. disputing and being relentlessly self-critical), but doesn't appear to be in the business of doing them in conjunction (being relentlessly self-critical about this disputing.)

Ribeiro goes on to claim that this is a "problem." A curious problem, indeed: What is the relationship between philosophy and disagreement?

Daniel Heller-Roazen has provided an account of what it is, following the Stoic percept, to live according to nature. He notes a distinction that "may seem subtle, but it is, in truth, of prime importance, as the thinkers of Antiquity well knew." Further,

> A text of uncertain authorship contained

in the *De anima liber cum mantissa* attributed to Alexander of Aphrodisias most clearly illustrates the point. The pertinent passage consists of two sentences, the first of which attributes a doctrine to some Stoics, "but not all of them": the belief, namely, that "that which the animal senses as the first thing that belongs [*to prōton oikeion*] is nothing other than itself." The second sentence continues: "Others, instead, seeking to give a more elegant and precise definition, say that from the moment of birth we are appropriated to our constitution and to that which preserves it [*phasin pros tēn sustasin kai tērēsin oikeiōsthai euthus genomenous hēmas tēn hēmōn autōn*]."

The contrast between the two statements could not be more clear. It sets a formulation of some imprecision against the principle repeatedly espoused by Seneca and the masters of the Stoic school. The 'more elegant and precise definition' posits, at the heart of every being, a difference without which it could not come to be itself: the difference between the self and its constitution, that most proper thing to which the animal, in relating itself to the world about it, comes by nature to be appropriated. Not the self but that to which the self perceives itself to be assigned

> and to which it must always adapt itself, the 'constitution' is that element within the animal with which it never altogether coincides, to which, from birth, it continues to 'conciliate' and 'commend' itself. It is that for which every living thing, to be and to preserve itself, must 'care,' that which each being, rational or not, incessantly senses and never knows.

Disagreement in philosophy follows from 'the difference,' in each philosopher, 'between the self and its constitution': That 'to which the self perceives itself to be assigned and to which it must always adapt itself,' what a philosopher must 'conciliate' him- or herself to before all else, and with every word, is the assignation of that self to inquiry. Mutually delivered over one to the other, mutually inexplicable one in terms of the other, everything in philosophy transpires between a self and the rigors of its inquiries. Investigation in its course, a kind of propitiation, is what comes to make one's inquiries, as it does one's life, as a philosopher, one's own. Informing every unaccountable departure, it is also that according to which philosophy lives. Brian Ribeiro, "Philosophy and Disagreement," *Crítica* 43 (2011): 3–4; Daniel Heller-Roazen, *The Inner Touch: Archaeology of a Sensation* (Cambridge, Mass.: Zone Books, 2007), 114–15.

References | 43

Pg. 7: an Art of Ignorance Giorgio Agamben, "The Last Chapter in the History of the World," in *Nudities*, trans. David Kishik and Stefan Pedatella (Stanford: Stanford University Press, 2011), 113–14.

Pg. 7: It is very difficult to say Deleuze, *Difference and Repetition*, xv. See also, at 162: "Problems are tests and selections."

Pg. 7: In the perusal of philosophical works Samuel Taylor Coleridge, *Biographia Literaria*, ed. Nigel Leask (New York: Everyman Paperbacks, 1997), 141.

Pg. 7: the status of the self-portrait Jacques Derrida, *Memoirs of the Blind: The Self-Portrait and Other Ruins*, trans. Pascale-Anne Brault and Michael Naas (Chicago: University of Chicago Press, 1993), 64.

Pg. 7: Even if one were sure Derrida, *Memoirs of the Blind*, 65.

Pg. 8: the inscription of the inscribable Derrida, *Memoirs of the Blind*, 45.

Pg. 9: an historical index Walter Benjamin, *The Arcades Project*, trans. Howard Eiland and Kevin McLaughlin (Cambridge, Mass.: Harvard University Press, 1999), 462–63. See 463 for "the perilous critical moment on which all reading is founded."

Pg. 9: It is more important that Alfred North Whitehead, *Process and Reality*, ed. David Ray Griffin and Donald W. Sherburne (New York: The Free Press, 1978), 259.

Pg. 9: the *Systema naturae*, Linnaeus assigns Giorgio Agamben, *The Open: Man and Animal*, trans. Kevin Attell (Stanford: Stanford University Press, 2004), 24.

Pg. 9: In truth, Linneaus' genius consists Agamben, *The Open*, 25.

Pg. 11: the notes for a reply Agamben, *The Open*, 26.

Pg. 11: a constitutively 'anthropomorphous' animal Agamben, *The Open*, 27.

Pg. 11: Hume only became who he is Walter Kaufmann, *Hegel: A Reinterpretation* (Notre Dame: University of Notre Dame Press, 1978), 278: "It would seem that the British discovered Hume's philosophical significance by way of Kant and Hegel." And higher up on the same page: "Berkeley and Hume had been prominently mentioned by Kant and could not be ignored. Through Kant they gained a place in the tradition."

Pg. 11: Hume asks how we know Quentin Meillassoux, "Potentiality and Virtuality," trans. Robin Mackay, in *The Speculative Turn: Continental Materialism and Realism*, eds. Levi Bryant, Nick Srnicek, and Graham Harman (Melbourne: re.press, 2011), 224–36.

Pg. 12: On the contrary, the ontological approach Meillassoux, "Potentiality and Virtuality," 226. See also, Quentin Meillassoux, *After Finitude: An Essay on the Necessity of Contingency*, trans. Ray Brassier (London: Continuum International Publishing Group, 2008), 84: "We all know the old adage according to which there is no absurdity that has not at one time or another been seriously defended by some philosopher. Our objector might acerbically remark that we have just proved this adage false, for there was one absurdity no one had yet proclaimed, and we have just unearthed it."

Pg. 12: I would affirm that, indeed Meillassoux, "Potentiality and Virtuality," 227.

Pg. 13: Žižek has pointed out Slavoj Žižek, "Is it Still Possible to be a Hegelian Today?" in *The Speculative Turn*, eds. Bryant, Srnicek, and Harman, 216.

Pg. 14: Umberto Eco has discussed this point Umberto Eco, "The Power of Falsehood," in *On Literature*, trans. Martin McLaughlin (New York: Harcourt Brace, 2004), 272–301. See also, 300: "The idea of the universe as the totality of the cosmos is an idea

> that comes from the most ancient cosmographies, cosmologies, and cosmogonies. But can we possibly describe, as if we could see it from above, something inside which we are con-tained, of which we form a part, and which we cannot leave? Can we provide a descriptive geometry of the universe when there is no space outside it onto which to project it? Can we speak of the beginning of the universe when a temporal notion like that of a beginning must refer to the parameters of a clock whereas at most the universe is its own clock and cannot be referred to anything that is external to it? Can we say with Eddington that 'hundreds of thousands of stars make up a galaxy; hundreds of thousands of galaxies make up the universe,' when, as [Jean-François] Gautier observes [in *L'Univers existe-t-il?*], although a galaxy is an object that can be observed, the universe is not, and therefore one is establishing an unwarranted analogy between two incommensurate entities?

Pg. 14: —what have I to do with refutations!— Friedrich Nietzsche, *On the Genealogy of Morals and Ecce Homo*, ed. Walter Kaufmann, trans. Walter Kaufmann and R.J. Hollingdale (New York: Random House, 1967), 18.

Pg. 14: as Deleuze and Guattari put it Gilles Deleuze and Felix Guattari, *A Thousand Plateaus: Capitalism and Schizophrenia*, trans. Brian Massumi (Minneapolis: University of Minnesota Press, 1987), 531: Lines of flight are "primary," they "are not phenomena of resistance or counterattack in an assemblage, but cutting edges of creation and deterritorialization."

Pg. 14: First you flee George Jackson, *Soledad Brother: The Prison Letters of George Jackson* (Chicago: Lawrence Hill Books, 1994), 328: "I may run, but all the time that I am, I'll be looking for a stick!"

Pg. 14: Philosophy is the invention Meillassoux, *After Finitude*, 76.

Pg. 15: Alexander Nehamas has staged Alexander Nehamas, *Nietzsche: Life as Literature* (Cambridge, Mass.: Harvard University Press, 1985), 34.

Pg. 16: Philosophy, like all other studies Bertrand Russell, *The Problems of Philosophy* (New York: Oxford University Press, 1959), 154–155.

Pg. 18: is exactly the same today Eric Dietrich, "There is No Progress in Philosophy," *Essays in Philosophy* 12:2 (2011): 332.

Pg. 18: Imagine that Aristotle Dietrich, "There is No Progress in Philosophy," 334.

Pg. 21: not exactly something that occurs Gilles Deleuze, *The Logic of Sense*, ed. Constantin V. Boundas, trans. Mark Lester with Charles Stivale (New York: Columbia University Press, 1990), 149 (my emphasis).

Pg. 21: the part that eludes Gilles Deleuze and Felix Guattari, *What is Philosophy?*, trans. Hugh Tomlinson and Graham Burchell (New York: Columbia University Press, 1994), 156. 111: "To think is to experiment,

> but experimentation is always that which is in the process of coming about—the new, remarkable, and interesting that replace the appearance of truth and are more demanding than it is. What is in the process of coming about is no more what ends than what begins. History is not experimentation, it is only the set of almost negative conditions

that make possible the experimentation of something that escapes history. Without history experimentation would remain indeterminate and unconditioned, but experimentation is not historical. It is philosophical.

Pg. 22: that is to say, acting counter Friedrich Nietzsche, *Untimely Meditations*, ed. Daniel Breazeale, trans. R. J. Hollingdale (New York: Cambridge University Press, 1997), 60. Alfred North Whitehead, *The Function of Reason* (Boston: Beacon Press, 1958), 80, 76: "The supremacy of fact over thought means that even the utmost flight of speculative thought should have its measure of truth": "Abstract speculation has been the salvation of the world—speculation which made systems and then transcended them, speculations which ventured to the furthest limit of abstraction. To set limits to speculation is treason to the future."

On Not Knowing

Pg. 22: What is meant in philosophy by the unknowable W.T. Stace, *The Philosophy of Hegel: A Systematic Exposition* (New York: Dover Publications, 1955), 46.

Pg. 22: If anything is unknowable Stace, *The Philosophy of Hegel*, 47.

Pg. 22: Total ignorance of a thing Stace, *The Philosophy of Hegel*, 47.

Pg. 23: an obscure passage of the *De Anima* Agamben, "On Potentiality," 184. Agamben claims of this passage, on the same page, "that it is truly one of the vertices of Aristotle's thought and that [it] fully authorizes the medieval image of a mystical Aristotle."

Pg. 24: All *potentia*, for Spinoza Gilles Deleuze, *Spinoza: Practical Philosophy*, trans. Robert Hurley (San Francisco: City Lights Books, 1988), 97.

Pg. 24: Potentiality is actual in perpetually separating from itself Gilles Deleuze, *The Logic of Sense*, trans. Mark Lester with Charles Stivale, ed. Constantin V. Boundas (New York: Columbia University Press, 1990), 151–52: "On one side, there is the part of the event which is realized and accomplished; on the other, there is that 'part of the event which cannot realize its accomplishment.' There are thus two accomplishments, which are like actualization, and counter-actualization."

Pg. 24: Maurice Merleau-Ponty speculates Heller-Roazen, *The Inner Touch*, 295–96.

Pg. 25: Heller-Roazen has provided a beautiful commentary Heller-Roazen, *The*

Inner Touch, 296.

Pg. 28: found in Plato's *Meno* Plato, *Five Dialogues*, trans. G.M.A. Grube (Indianapolis: Hackett Publishing Company, Inc., 1981), 69.

Pg. 28: the Socratic enterprise See Alexander Nehamas, *The Art of Living: Socratic Reflections from Plato to Foucault* (Berkeley: University of California Press, 2000). See also Brian Satterfield, "What is the Good of the 'Examined Life'? Some Thoughts on the *Apology* and Liberal Education," *Expositions* 3.2 (2009): 183–84:

> [T]o say that the reason for examining one's life is not to misspend it is to miss the more problematic dimension of Socrates' claim; it is to transform Socrates' practice into an essentially utilitarian activity, good because of its possible benefits or outcomes. It is to trivialize Socratic philosophy by turning it into a species of self-help. Having reflected and come to better views of what one ought to aim at, it implies, we should set aside reflection and examination, and go on with leading our new, more meaningful lives. So seen, reflection may be a necessary preliminary—especially in corrupt places and times—but it is ultimately only a preparation for life, not life itself.

Socrates' own words are more challenging, and for two reasons. The first is that thinking things over seems to be, for Socrates, not a means to an end, but an end itself. It is, he says—astonishingly—not the *practice* of virtue that is the greatest good for a human being, but *talking about* virtue in the course of every day. This proposition is only defensible, I suggest, if talking about virtue *is* virtue. Virtue, Socrates seems to be suggesting, is necessarily actively self-reflective, the eye seeing itself seeing. Something about this tends to stick in the craw of students. For not only do many of them not see themselves as especially interested in thinking, but the demands that Socrates seems to place on them—that they suspend concerns for advancement, family, and personal lives while they enter upon a course of questioning that will ultimately prove inconclusive—seem extreme, even perverse. The natural tendency is to dismiss by becoming 'reasonable,' temporizing. Sure, some reflection is good; but Socrates takes it too far. 'Shouldn't he be supporting his children?' is a common question.

Reinforcing this objection is a second: if Socrates himself is a model of the kind of examination that he urges on others, his lifetime of inquiry appears remarkably unsuccessful. Having constantly engaged in discussions about virtue, he seems by the time of his trial to have learned nothing. All he has achieved, on his own account, is knowledge of his ignorance. The prospect of spending one's life in unpleasant (as students think) and fruitless inquiry—inquiry which does not even pretend to hold out the possibility of answers—is disheartening. And some, understandably enough, lose interest as soon as it becomes clear that there is no concrete prize or reward at the end. The natural question of the student—'what am I going to get out of this?'—has no answer that the soul disposed to ask it in the first place is going to recognize as satisfactory; reflection and self-knowledge are not products, but processes, or rather activities. One does not, in thinking about Socratic questions, typically get a final answer; one gets—at best—understanding of possibilities.

Pg. 29: Kant distinguishes between Agamben, "On Potentiality," 214. See also A 761 / B 789 in Immanuel Kant, *Critique of Pure Reason*, trans. Werner S. Pluhar (Indianapolis: Hackett Publishing Company, Inc., 1996), 703.

Pg. 30: Agamben has discussed the manner Agamben, *The Open*, 13–14.

Pg. 32: as what results from the incongruity Agamben, *The Open*, 16.

References

Agamben, Giorgio. *Homo Sacer: Sovereign Power and Bare Life*. Trans. Daniel Heller-Roazen. Stanford: Stanford University Press, 1998.

---. *Nudities*. Trans. David Kishik and Stefan Pedatella. Stanford: Stanford University Press, 2011.

---. *The Open: Man and Animal*. Trans. Kevin Attell. Stanford: Stanford University Press, 2004.

---. *Potentialities: Collected Essays in Philosophy*. Ed. and trans. Daniel Heller-Roazen. Stanford: Stanford University Press, 1999.

Auden. W.H. *Collected Poems: Auden*. Ed. Edward Mendelson. New York: Vintage, 1991.

Barthes, Roland. *The Neutral*. Trans. Rosalind E. Krauss and Denis Hollier. New York: Columbia University Press, 2005.

Benjamin, Walter. *The Arcades Project*. Trans. Howard Eiland and Kevin McLaughlin. Cambridge, Mass.: Harvard University Press, 1999.

Bryant, Levi, Nick Srnicek, and Graham Harman, eds. *The Speculative Turn: Continental Materialism and Realism*. Melbourne: re.press, 2011.

Coleridge, Samuel Taylor. *Biographia Literaria*. Ed. Nigel Leask. London: Everyman Paperbacks, 1997.

Deleuze, Gilles. *Difference and Repetition*. Trans. Paul Patton. New York: Columbia University Press, 1994.

---. *The Logic of Sense*. Trans. Mark Lester with Charles Stivale. Ed. Constantin V. Boundas. New York: Columbia University Press, 1990.

---. *Spinoza: Practical Philosophy*. Trans. Robert Hurley. San Francisco: City Lights Books, 1988.

Deleuze, Gilles and Felix Guattari. *A Thousand Plateaus: Capitalism and Schizophrenia*. Trans. Brian Massumi. Minneapolis: University of Minnesota Press, 1987.

---. *What is Philosophy?* Trans. Hugh Tomlinson and Graham Burchell. New York: Columbia University Press, 1994.

Derrida, Jacques. *Memoirs of the Blind: The Self-Portrait and Other Ruins*. Trans. Pascale-Anne Brault and Michael Naas. Chicago: University of Chicago Press, 1993.

Dietrich, Eric. "There is No Progress in Philosophy." *Essays in Philosophy* 12:2 (2011): 329-344.

Eco, Umberto. *On Literature*. Trans. Martin McLaughlin. New York: Harcourt Brace, 2004.

Harman, Graham. *Quentin Meillassoux: Philosophy in the Making*. Edinburgh: Edinburgh University Press, 2011.

Heller-Roazen, Daniel. *The Inner Touch: Archaeology of a Sensation*. Cambridge, Mass.: Zone Books, 2007.

Jackson, George. *Soledad Brother: The Prison Letters of George Jackson*. Chicago: Lawrence Hill Books, 1994.

Kant, Immanuel. *Critique of Pure Reason*. Trans. Werner S. Pluhar. Indianapolis: Hackett Publishing Company, Inc., 1996.

Kaufmann, Walter. *Hegel: A Reinterpretation.* Notre Dame: University of Notre Dame Press, 1978.

Meillassoux, Quentin. *After Finitude: And Essay on the Necessity of Contingency.* Trans. Ray Brassier. London: Continuum International Publishing Group, 2008.

Nehemas, Alexander. *Nietzsche: Life as Literature.* Cambridge, Mass.: Harvard University Press, 1985.

---. *The Art of Living: Socratic Reflections from Plato to Foucault.* Berkeley: University of California Press, 2000.

Nietzsche, Friedrich. *On the Genealogy of Morals and Ecce Homo.* Ed. Walter Kaufmann. Trans. Walter Kaufmann and R.J. Hollingdale. New York: Random House, 1967.

---. *Untimely* Meditations. Ed. Daniel Breazeale. Trans. R. J. Hollingdale. New York: Cambridge University Press, 1997.

Plato, *Five Dialogues.* Trans. G.M.A. Grube. Indianapolis: Hackett Publishing Company, Inc., 1981.

Ribeiro, Brian. "Philosophy and Disagreement." *Crítica* 43 (2011): 3–25.

Russell, Bertrand. *The Problems of Philosophy*. New York: Oxford University Press, 1959.

Satterfield, Brian. "What is the Good of the 'Examined Life'? Some Thoughts on the *Apology* and Liberal Education." *Expositions* 3.2 (2009): 173–184.

Spinoza, Baruch. *Ethics, Treatise on the Emendation of the Intellect, and Selected Letters*. Ed. Seymour Feldman. Trans. Samuel Shirley. Indianapolis: Hackett Publishing Company, Inc., 1992.

Stace, W.T. *The Philosophy of Hegel: A Systematic Exposition*. New York: Dover Publications, 1955.

Whitehead, Alfred North. *The Function of Reason*. Boston: Beacon Press, 1958.

---. *Process and Reality*. Eds. David Ray Griffin and Donald W. Sherburne. New York: The Free Press, 1978.

W. dreams, like Phaedrus, of an army of thinker-friends, thinker-lovers. He dreams of a thought-army, a thought-pack, which would storm the philosophical Houses of Parliament.He dreams of Tartars from the philosophical steppes, of thought-barbarians, thought-outsiders. What distances would shine in their eyes!

~Lars Iyer

www.babelworkinggroup.org

WHAT IS PHILOSOPHY?

BETWEEN LOVE AND WISDOM

www.ingramcontent.com/pod-product-compliance
Lightning Source LLC
Chambersburg PA
CBHW070849160426
43192CB00012B/2373